thai **dishes**

Easy dishes to cook at home

First published in 2009
Love Food ® is an imprint of Parragon Books Ltd

Parragon
Queen Street House
4 Queen Street
Bath BA1 1HE, UK

ISBN: 978-1-4075-8106-4

Printed in Malaysia

Designed by Talking Design

Notes for the reader
This book uses imperial, metric, and US cup measurements. Follow the same units of measurement throughout; do not mix imperial and metric. All spoon measurements are level: teaspoons are assumed to be 5 ml, and tablespoons are assumed to be 15 ml. Unless otherwise stated, milk is assumed to be whole, eggs and individual vegetables, such as potatoes, are medium, and pepper is freshly ground black pepper.

The times given are an approximate guide only. Preparation times differ according to the techniques used by different people and the cooking times may also vary from those given as a result of the type of oven used. Optional ingredients, variations, or serving suggestions have not been included in the calculations.

Recipes using raw or very lightly cooked eggs should be avoided by infants, the elderly, pregnant women, convalescents, and anyone with a chronic condition. Pregnant and breastfeeding women are advised to avoid eating peanuts and peanut products. People with nut allergies should be aware that some of the prepared ingredients used in the recipes in this book may contain nuts. Always check the packaging before use.

Contents

introduction

The cuisine of Thailand has become increasingly popular in the Western world in recent years. Thai food is exotic and vibrant with intense, fresh flavors that tantalize the taste buds. It is full of variety with its array of colors, flavors, and textures. Dishes can range from hot and spicy with red or green chiles, sharp with kaffir lime leaves, or deliciously creamy with coconut and coconut milk.

Having been largely unexplored in its past, Thailand is now an increasingly popular travelers' destination. Nestled between China and India, it has become steeped in the influences of both. The first settlers in Thailand are thought to have been from Southern China and it was they who introduced the techniques of stir-frying and steaming that are now so widely practiced in the Thai kitchen.

The distinctive flavors of Thai cooking (primarily sweet, spicy, sour, bitter, and salty) used to be difficult to reproduce because authentic ingredients weren't widely available. This, however, is a thing of the past with many supermarkets now stocking not only Thai staples, such as jasmine rice, rice noodles, and fish sauce, but also lesser known ingredients, including galangal and Thai basil. Prepared Thai curry pastes are widely available but, if you prefer, they can also be made at home following these easy recipes:

Thai Red Curry Paste

1 tbsp coriander seeds
1 tbsp cumin seeds
12 dried red chiles, chopped
2 shallots, chopped
6 garlic cloves, chopped
1-inch/2.5-cm piece fresh ginger, chopped
2 lemongrass stalks, chopped
4 fresh kaffir lime leaves, chopped
handful of fresh cilantro, chopped
finely grated rind of 1 lime
1 tsp salt
1 tsp black peppercorns, crushed

Heat a dry skillet until hot, add the coriander and cumin seeds, and cook over medium–high heat, shaking the skillet frequently, for 2–3 minutes, or until starting to pop. Put the toasted seeds with all the remaining ingredients in a food processor or small blender and process to a thick, smooth paste.

Thai Green Curry Paste

1 tbsp coriander seeds
1 tbsp cumin seeds
12 fresh green bird's eye chiles, chopped
5 garlic cloves, chopped
2 lemongrass stalks, chopped
5 fresh kaffir lime leaves, chopped
handful of fresh cilantro, chopped
finely grated rind of 1 lime
1 tsp salt
1 tsp black peppercorns, crushed

Heat a dry skillet until hot, add the coriander and cumin seeds, and cook over medium–high heat, shaking the skillet frequently, for 2–3 minutes, or until starting to pop. Put the toasted seeds with all the remaining ingredients in a food processor or small blender and process to a thick, smooth paste.

Mussaman Curry Paste

4 large dried red chiles
2 tsp shrimp paste
3 shallots, finely chopped
3 garlic cloves, finely chopped
1-inch/2.5-cm piece fresh galangal, chopped
2 lemongrass stalks, chopped
2 cloves
1 tbsp coriander seeds
1 tbsp cumin seeds
seeds from 2 green cardamom pods
1 tsp black peppercorns
1 tsp salt

Cut off and discard the chile stalks and place the chiles in a bowl. Cover with hot water and soak for 30–45 minutes. Wrap the shrimp paste in foil and broil or dry-fry for 2–3 minutes, turning once or twice. Remove from the broiler or skillet. Dry-fry the shallots, garlic, galangal, lemongrass, cloves, and coriander, cumin, and cardamom seeds over low heat, stirring frequently, for 3–4 minutes, until lightly browned. Transfer to a food processor and process until finely ground. Add the chiles and their soaking water and the peppercorns and salt, and process again. Add the shrimp paste and process again to a smooth paste.

light **bites**

Hot & Sour Soup

SERVES 4

2 fresh red chiles, seeded and coarsely chopped
6 tbsp rice vinegar
5 cups vegetable stock
2 lemongrass stalks, halved
4 tbsp soy sauce
1 tbsp jaggery or light brown sugar
juice of ½ lime
2 tbsp peanut or vegetable oil
8 oz/225 g firm tofu (drained weight), cut into ½-inch/1-cm cubes
14 oz/400 g canned straw mushrooms, drained
4 scallions, chopped
1 small head of bok choy, shredded
handful of fresh cilantro leaves

Mix the chiles and vinegar together in a nonmetallic bowl. Cover and let stand at room temperature for 1 hour. Meanwhile, bring the stock to a boil in a pan. Add the lemongrass, soy sauce, jaggery, and lime juice, then reduce the heat and simmer for 20–30 minutes.

Heat the oil in a preheated wok, then add the tofu and stir-fry over high heat for 2–3 minutes, or until browned all over. (You may need to do this in 2 batches, depending on the size of the wok.) Remove with a slotted spoon and drain on paper towels.

Add the chiles and vinegar to the stock mixture together with the tofu, mushrooms, and half the scallions and cook for 10 minutes. Mix the remaining scallions with the bok choy and cilantro, and sprinkle over the soup before serving.

Vegetable & Black Bean *Egg Rolls*

SERVES 4

- 2 tbsp peanut or vegetable oil, plus extra for deep-frying
- 4 scallions, cut into 2-inch/5-cm lengths and shredded lengthwise, plus extra to garnish
- 1-inch/2.5-cm piece fresh ginger, finely chopped
- 1 large carrot, cut into thin sticks
- 1 red bell pepper, seeded and cut into thin sticks
- 6 tbsp black bean sauce
- 1/3 cup fresh bean sprouts
- 7 oz/200 g canned water chestnuts, drained and coarsely chopped
- 2-inch/5-cm piece cucumber, cut into thin sticks
- 8 x 8-inch/20-cm square egg roll skins
- sweet chili dipping sauce, to serve (optional)

Heat the 2 tablespoons of oil in a preheated wok. Add the scallions, ginger, carrot, and bell pepper, then stir-fry over medium–high heat for 2–3 minutes. Add the black bean sauce, bean sprouts, water chestnuts, and cucumber and stir-fry for 1–2 minutes. Let cool.

Remove the egg roll skins from the package, but keep them in a pile, and cover with plastic wrap to prevent them from drying out. Lay one skin on a counter in front of you in a diamond shape and brush the edges with water. Put a spoonful of the filling near one corner and fold the corner over the filling. Roll over again and then fold the side corners over the filling. Roll up to enclose the filling completely. Repeat with the remaining skins and filling.

Heat the oil for deep-frying in a wok, deep pan, or deep-fat fryer to 350–375°F/ 180–190°C, or until a cube of bread browns in 30 seconds. Add the egg rolls, in 2–3 batches, and cook for 2–3 minutes, or until crisp and golden all over. Remove with a slotted spoon and drain on paper towels, then keep warm while you cook the remaining egg rolls. Garnish with shredded scallions and serve with sweet chili dipping sauce, if using.

Chicken Satay Skewers
with Peanut Sauce

SERVES 4

4 skinless, boneless chicken breasts, about 4 oz/115 g each, cut into 3/4-inch/2-cm cubes
4 tbsp soy sauce
1 tbsp cornstarch
2 garlic cloves, finely chopped
1-inch/2.5-cm piece fresh ginger, finely chopped
diced cucumber, to serve

Peanut sauce

2 tbsp peanut or vegetable oil
1/2 onion, finely chopped
1 garlic clove, finely chopped
4 tbsp crunchy peanut butter
4–5 tbsp water
1/2 tsp chili powder

Put the chicken in a shallow dish. Mix the soy sauce, cornstarch, garlic, and ginger together in a small bowl and pour over the chicken. Cover and let marinate in the refrigerator for at least 2 hours.

Meanwhile, soak 12 wooden skewers in cold water for at least 30 minutes. Preheat the oven to 375°F/190°C. Divide the chicken cubes among the skewers.

Heat a ridged grill pan until hot, then add the skewers and cook over high heat for 3–4 minutes, turning occasionally, until browned all over. Transfer the skewers to a baking sheet and cook in the preheated oven for 5–8 minutes, or until cooked through.

Meanwhile, to make the sauce, heat the oil in a pan, then add the onion and garlic and cook over medium heat, stirring frequently, for 3–4 minutes, or until softened. Add the peanut butter, water, and chili powder and simmer for 2–3 minutes, or until softened and thinned. Serve the skewers immediately with the warm sauce and the cucumber.

Crab, Pork & Chile
Fritters

SERVES 4

Fritters

4 oz/115 g canned white crabmeat, drained
4 oz/115 g fresh ground pork
2 fresh red chiles, seeded and coarsely chopped
1 tsp salt
2 scallions, chopped
handful of fresh cilantro, chopped
1 egg white
peanut or vegetable oil, for pan-frying

Dipping sauce

2/3 cup water
4 tbsp superfine sugar
1 tbsp rice vinegar
1/2 small red onion, very finely diced
2-inch/5-cm piece cucumber, very finely diced

Put all the fritter ingredients except the oil in a food processor and process to a coarse paste. Use damp hands to shape into 20 small, flat patties.

Heat enough oil to cover the bottom of a large skillet. Add the fritters, in 2–3 batches, and cook over medium–high heat for 2 minutes on each side, or until browned and cooked through. Remove with a slotted spoon and drain on paper towels, then keep warm while you cook the remaining fritters.

Meanwhile, to make the dipping sauce, put the water, sugar, and vinegar in a small pan and heat gently until the sugar has dissolved. Add the onion and cucumber and simmer for 5 minutes. Serve the fritters hot with the dipping sauce.

Crispy Pork
Dumplings

SERVES 4

- 5 small fresh red chiles
- 3 scallions, coarsely chopped
- 1 garlic clove, coarsely chopped
- 9 oz/250 g fresh ground pork
- 1 tsp salt
- 20 wonton skins
- peanut or vegetable oil, for deep-frying

To make the chile flowers for the garnish, use a sharp knife to make 6–8 slits about ½ inch/1 cm from the stem end to the tip of 4 of the chiles. Put them into a bowl of ice water and let soak for 30 minutes, until they have expanded into flower shapes.

To make the dumplings, seed and coarsely chop the remaining chile, then put it into a food processor with the scallions, garlic, pork, and salt and process to a smooth paste.

Remove the wonton skins from the package, but keep them in a pile, and cover with plastic wrap to prevent them from drying out. Lay one skin on a counter in front of you in a diamond shape and brush the edges with water. Put a small amount of filling near one edge and fold the skin over the filling. Press the edges together to seal the pocket and shape into a semicircle. Repeat with the remaining skins and filling.

Heat the oil in a wok, deep pan, or deep-fat fryer to 350–375°F/180–190°C, or until a cube of bread browns in 30 seconds. Add the dumplings, in batches, and cook for 45 seconds–1 minute, or until crisp and golden all over. Remove with a slotted spoon and drain on paper towels, then keep warm while you cook the remaining dumplings. Serve immediately once they are all cooked, garnished with the chile flowers.

Shrimp
Wraps

SERVES 4

24 cooked jumbo shrimp, peeled and tails left intact
2 tbsp sweet chili dipping sauce
24 wonton skins
peanut or vegetable oil, for deep-frying

Dipping sauce

1 tbsp sesame oil
3 tbsp soy sauce
½-inch/1-cm piece fresh ginger, finely chopped
1 scallion, finely chopped

Toss the shrimp in the chili sauce in a bowl. Remove the wonton skins from the package, but keep them in a pile, and cover with plastic wrap to prevent them from drying out. Lay one skin on a counter in front of you and brush the edges with water. Place a shrimp diagonally across the square and fold the skin around the shrimp to enclose it, leaving the tail sticking out. Repeat with the remaining skins and shrimp.

Heat the oil for deep-frying in a wok, deep pan, or deep-fat fryer to 350–375°F/180–190°C, or until a cube of bread browns in 30 seconds. Add the wraps, in batches, and cook for 45 seconds–1 minute, or until crisp and golden all over. Remove with a slotted spoon and drain on paper towels, then keep warm while you cook the remaining wraps.

Meanwhile, to make the dipping sauce, mix together the sesame oil, soy sauce, ginger, and scallion in a bowl. Serve in a small serving bowl with the wraps.

Crab
Wontons

SERVES 4

- 1 tbsp peanut or vegetable oil, plus extra for deep-frying
- 1-inch/2.5-cm piece fresh ginger, finely chopped
- 1/4 red bell pepper, seeded and finely chopped
- handful of fresh cilantro, chopped
- 1/4 tsp salt
- 5 1/2 oz/150 g canned white crabmeat, drained
- 20 wonton skins
- soy sauce or sweet chili dipping sauce, to serve

Heat the 1 tablespoon of oil in a preheated wok, then add the ginger and bell pepper and stir-fry over high heat for 30 seconds. Add the cilantro and mix well. Let cool, then add the salt and crabmeat and mix well.

Remove the wonton skins from the package, but keep them in a pile, and cover with plastic wrap to prevent them from drying out. Lay one skin on a counter in front of you and brush the edges with water. Put a teaspoonful of the crabmeat mixture in the center and fold the skin over the mixture to form a triangle. Press the edges together to seal. Fold each side corner up to the top corner to make a small pocket, brushing the edges with water to seal if necessary. Repeat with the remaining skins and crabmeat mixture.

Heat the oil for deep-frying in a wok, deep pan, or deep-fat fryer to 350–375°F/180–190°C, or until a cube of bread browns in 30 seconds. Add the wontons, in batches, and cook for 45 seconds–1 minute, or until crisp and golden all over. Remove with a slotted spoon and drain on paper towels, then keep warm while you cook the remaining wontons. Serve with soy sauce or sweet chili dipping sauce.

meat & **poultry dishes**

Pad Thai

Noodles

SERVES 4

8 oz/225 g thin rice noodles
3/4 cup coarsely chopped peanuts
2 tbsp lime juice
1 tbsp superfine sugar
6 tbsp Thai fish sauce
1 tsp hot chili sauce, or to taste
9 oz/250 g firm tofu (drained weight), cubed
3 tbsp peanut or vegetable oil, plus extra for deep-frying
1 garlic clove, crushed
1 onion, finely sliced
1 red bell pepper, seeded and thinly sliced
9 oz/250 g skinless, boneless chicken breast, cut into thin strips
1/2 cup fresh bean sprouts
4 1/2 oz/125 g snow peas
6 oz/175 g cooked peeled shrimp, cut in half lengthwise
3 eggs, beaten

Soak the noodles in a bowl of warm water for 10–15 minutes or according to the package directions, until tender. Drain thoroughly in a colander and set aside. Mix together the peanuts, lime juice, sugar, fish sauce, and hot chili sauce in a small bowl and set aside.

Rinse the tofu in cold water, place between layers of paper towels, and pat dry. Heat the oil for deep-frying in a wok, deep pan, or deep-fat fryer to 180–190°C/350–375°F, or until a cube of bread browns in 30 seconds. Add the tofu and cook for 2 minutes, until light brown and crisp. Remove from the heat, lift the tofu out with a slotted spoon, and let drain thoroughly on paper towels.

Heat a large skillet or wok and add the 3 tablespoons of oil, the garlic, onion, bell pepper, and chicken. Cook for 2–3 minutes. Stir in the bean sprouts and snow peas and cook for 1 minute, then add the shrimp, noodles, eggs, and tofu and stir-fry for an additional 4–5 minutes. Finally, add the peanut-and-lime juice mixture and cook for 3–4 minutes. Transfer to warmed dishes and serve.

Thai Green
Chicken Curry

SERVES 4

2 tbsp peanut oil or corn oil
2 tbsp Thai green curry paste
1 lb 2 oz/500 g skinless, boneless chicken breasts, cut into cubes
2 kaffir lime leaves, coarsely torn
1 lemongrass stalk, finely chopped
1 cup coconut milk
16 baby eggplants, halved
2 tbsp Thai fish sauce
fresh Thai basil sprigs and thinly sliced kaffir lime leaves, to garnish

Heat the oil in a preheated wok or large, heavy-bottom skillet. Add the curry paste and stir-fry briefly until all the aromas are released.

Add the chicken, lime leaves, and lemongrass and stir-fry for 3–4 minutes, until the meat is beginning to color. Add the coconut milk and eggplants and simmer gently for 8–10 minutes, or until tender.

Stir in the fish sauce and serve immediately garnished with Thai basil sprigs and lime leaves.

Warm Noodle Salad
with Gingered Chicken

SERVES 4

4 scallions, chopped
1-inch/2.5-cm piece fresh ginger, finely chopped
2 garlic cloves, crushed
2 tbsp vegetable or peanut oil
4 skinless, boneless chicken breasts, cut into 1-inch/2.5-cm cubes

Salad

1–2 tbsp vegetable or peanut oil
1 onion, sliced
2 garlic cloves, chopped
4 oz/115 g baby corn, halved lengthwise
1½ cups snow peas, halved diagonally
1 red bell pepper, seeded and sliced
3-inch/7.5-cm piece cucumber, peeled, seeded, and sliced
4 tbsp Thai soy sauce
1 tbsp jaggery or light brown sugar
a few fresh Thai basil leaves
6 oz/175 g fine egg noodles

Mix the scallions, ginger, garlic, and the 2 tablespoons of oil together in a shallow dish and add the chicken. Cover and let marinate for at least 3 hours. Lift the meat out of the marinade and set aside.

Heat 1 tablespoon of the remaining oil in a wok and cook the onion for 1–2 minutes before adding the garlic, baby corn, snow peas, and bell pepper. Cook for 2–3 minutes, until just tender. Add the cucumber, half the soy sauce, the jaggery, and basil, and mix gently.

Cook the noodles in a large pan of boiling water for 4 minutes or according to the package directions, until just tender. Drain well. Sprinkle over the remaining soy sauce and arrange on serving plates. Top with the cooked vegetables.

Add the remaining oil to the wok, if necessary, and cook the chicken over high heat until browned on all sides. Arrange the chicken on top of the salad and serve hot or warm.

Mussaman

Curry

SERVES 4

2 tbsp peanut or vegetable oil
8 oz/225 g shallots, coarsely chopped
1 garlic clove, crushed
1 lb/450 g beef tenderloin, thickly sliced and cut into 1-inch/2.5-cm cubes
2 tbsp Mussaman curry paste
3 potatoes, cut into 1-inch/2.5-cm cubes
1 3/4 cups coconut milk
2 tbsp soy sauce
2/3 cup beef stock
1 tsp jaggery or light brown sugar
1/2 cup unsalted peanuts
handful of fresh cilantro, chopped
freshly cooked noodles, to serve

Heat the oil in a preheated wok. Add the shallots and garlic and stir-fry over medium–high heat for 1–2 minutes, or until softened. Add the beef and curry paste and stir-fry over high heat for 2–3 minutes, or until browned all over.

Add the potatoes, coconut milk, soy sauce, stock, and jaggery and bring gently to a boil, stirring occasionally. Reduce the heat and simmer for 8–10 minutes, or until the potatoes are tender.

Meanwhile, heat a dry skillet until hot, then add the peanuts and cook over medium–high heat, shaking the skillet frequently, for 2–3 minutes, or until lightly browned. Add to the curry with the cilantro and stir well. Serve hot with noodles.

Red Curry Pork
with Bell Peppers

SERVES 4–6

- 2 tbsp peanut or vegetable oil
- 1 onion, coarsely chopped
- 2 garlic cloves, chopped
- 1 lb/450 g pork tenderloin, thickly sliced
- 1 red bell pepper, seeded and cut into chunks
- 6 oz/175 g button mushrooms, quartered
- 2 tbsp Thai red curry paste
- 2½ cups coconut cream
- 1 tsp pork or vegetable bouillon powder
- 2 tbsp Thai soy sauce
- 4 tomatoes, peeled, seeded, and chopped
- handful of fresh cilantro, chopped

Heat the oil in a wok or large skillet and sauté the onion and garlic for 1–2 minutes, until they are softened but not browned. Add the pork and stir-fry for 2–3 minutes, until browned all over. Add the bell pepper, mushrooms, and curry paste.

Add the coconut cream to the wok with the bouillon powder and soy sauce. Bring to a boil and let simmer for 4–5 minutes, until the liquid has reduced and thickened. Add the tomatoes and most of the cilantro and cook for 1–2 minutes. Sprinkle with the remaining cilantro and serve immediately.

Red Roasted Pork
with Peppered Noodles

SERVES 2

- 1 tbsp Thai red curry paste
- 2 tbsp soy sauce
- 12 oz/350 g pork tenderloin, trimmed
- 8 oz/225 g fine egg noodles
- 2 tbsp peanut or vegetable oil
- 1 red onion, chopped
- 1-inch/2.5-cm piece fresh ginger, finely chopped
- 1 garlic clove, finely chopped
- 1 orange bell pepper, seeded and chopped
- 1 red bell pepper, seeded and chopped
- 1 tbsp black pepper
- small bunch of fresh chives, snipped
- handful of fresh cilantro, chopped

Mix the curry paste and soy sauce together in a small bowl and spread over the pork tenderloin. Cover and let marinate in the refrigerator for 1 hour.

Preheat the oven to 400°F/200°C. Roast the pork in the preheated oven for 20–25 minutes, or until cooked through. Remove from the oven, then cover with foil and let rest for 15 minutes.

Meanwhile, cook the noodles in a large pan of boiling water for 4 minutes or according to the package directions, until just tender. Drain, then rinse under cold running water and set aside.

Heat the oil in a preheated wok. Add the onion, ginger, and garlic and stir-fry over medium–high heat for 1–2 minutes. Add the orange and red bell peppers and black pepper and stir-fry for 2–3 minutes, or until tender. Stir in the chives and most of the cilantro.

Add the drained noodles to the bell pepper mixture and toss together until well mixed. Divide between 2 serving dishes. Slice the pork and arrange on top of the noodles. Sprinkle with the remaining cilantro and serve immediately.

fish & **seafood dishes**

Squid & Shrimp
Laksa

SERVES 4

- 8 oz/225 g thick rice noodles
- 3 cups coconut milk
- 2 fish stock cubes
- 3 fresh kaffir lime leaves
- 2 tbsp Thai red curry paste
- 1 bunch of scallions, coarsely chopped
- 2 fresh red chiles, seeded and coarsely chopped
- 8 oz/225 g raw squid, cleaned and cut into rings
- 8 oz/225 g large raw shrimp, peeled and deveined
- handful of fresh cilantro, chopped, plus extra leaves to garnish

Place the noodles in a pan of boiling water, cover, and let soak for 4 minutes or according to the packet instructions, until just tender. Drain, then rinse under cold running water and set aside.

Put the coconut milk, stock cubes, lime leaves, curry paste, scallions, and chiles in a large pan and bring gently to a boil, stirring occasionally. Reduce the heat and simmer, stirring occasionally, for 2–3 minutes, or until the stock cubes and curry paste have dissolved.

Add the squid and shrimp and simmer for 1–2 minutes, or until the squid has plumped up and the shrimp have turned pink. Add the cooked noodles and the chopped cilantro and stir well. Serve in soup bowls, garnished with cilantro leaves.

Thai Fish
Curry

SERVES 4

- juice of 1 lime
- 4 tbsp Thai fish sauce
- 2 tbsp Thai soy sauce
- 1 fresh red chile, seeded and chopped
- 12 oz/350 g monkfish fillet, cut into cubes
- 12 oz/350 g salmon fillet, skinned and cut into cubes
- 1¾ cups coconut milk
- 3 kaffir lime leaves
- 1 tbsp Thai red curry paste
- 1 lemongrass stalk (white part only), finely chopped
- freshly cooked jasmine rice and chopped fresh cilantro, to serve

Combine the lime juice, half the fish sauce, and the soy sauce in a shallow, nonmetallic dish. Add the chile and fish and stir to coat. Cover with plastic wrap and chill in the refrigerator for 1–2 hours, or overnight.

Bring the coconut milk to a boil in a pan and add the lime leaves, curry paste, the remaining fish sauce, and the lemongrass. Let simmer gently for 10–15 minutes.

Add the fish with its marinade and let simmer for 4–5 minutes, until the fish is cooked. Serve hot, accompanied by jasmine rice with chopped cilantro stirred through it.

Mixed Seafood
Curry

SERVES 4

1 tbsp vegetable or peanut oil
3 shallots, finely chopped
1-inch/2.5-cm piece fresh galangal, thinly sliced
2 garlic cloves, finely chopped
1¾ cups coconut milk
2 lemongrass stalks, broken in half
4 tbsp Thai fish sauce
2 tbsp chili sauce
8 oz/225 g raw jumbo shrimp, peeled and deveined
8 oz/225 g baby squid, cleaned and thickly sliced
8 oz/225 g salmon fillet, skinned and cut into chunks
6 oz/175 g tuna steak, cut into chunks
8 oz/225 g mussels, scrubbed and debearded
lime wedges, to garnish
freshly cooked rice, to serve

Heat the oil in a large wok with a tight-fitting lid and stir-fry the shallots, galangal, and garlic for 1–2 minutes, until they start to soften. Add the coconut milk, lemongrass, fish sauce, and chili sauce. Bring to a boil, reduce the heat, and let simmer for 1–2 minutes.

Add the shrimp, squid, salmon, and tuna, and simmer for 3–4 minutes, until the shrimp have turned pink and the fish is cooked.

Discard any mussels with broken shells and any that refuse to close when tapped with a knife. Add the remaining mussels to the wok and cover with a lid. Let simmer for 1–2 minutes, until they have opened. Discard any mussels that remain closed. Garnish with lime wedges and serve immediately with rice.

Stir-Fried Salmon & Scallops
with Cilantro & Lime

SERVES 4

6 tbsp peanut oil
10 oz/280 g salmon steak, skinned and cut into 1-inch/2.5-cm chunks
8 oz/225 g prepared scallops
3 carrots, thinly sliced
2 celery stalks, cut into 1-inch/2.5-cm pieces
2 yellow bell peppers, seeded and thinly sliced
3 cups oyster mushrooms, thinly sliced
1 garlic clove, crushed
6 tbsp chopped fresh cilantro
3 shallots, thinly sliced
juice of 2 limes
1 tsp grated lime rind
1 tsp dried red pepper flakes
3 tbsp dry sherry
3 tbsp soy sauce

Heat the oil in a preheated wok. Add the salmon and scallops, and stir-fry for 3 minutes. Remove from the wok, then set aside and keep warm.

Add the carrots, celery, bell peppers, mushrooms, and garlic to the wok and stir-fry for 3 minutes. Add the cilantro and shallots, and stir.

Stir in the lime juice and rind, dried red pepper flakes, sherry, and soy sauce and stir. Return the salmon and scallops to the wok and stir-fry carefully for an additional minute. Serve immediately.

Chili Shrimp
with Garlic Noodles

SERVES 4

7 oz/200 g cooked jumbo shrimp, peeled and tails left intact
4 tbsp sweet chili dipping sauce
4 tbsp peanut or vegetable oil
4 scallions, chopped
2 oz/55 g snow peas, trimmed and halved diagonally
1 tbsp Thai red curry paste
1¾ cups coconut milk
4 oz/115 g canned bamboo shoots, drained
⅓ cup fresh bean sprouts

Garlic noodles

4 oz/115 g medium egg noodles
2 garlic cloves, crushed
handful of fresh cilantro, chopped
salt

Toss the shrimp with the chili sauce in a bowl. Cover and set aside. Heat half the oil in a preheated wok. Add the scallions and snow peas, then stir-fry over medium–high heat for 2–3 minutes. Add the curry paste and stir well. Pour in the coconut milk and bring gently to a boil, stirring occasionally.

Add the bamboo shoots and bean sprouts and cook, stirring, for 1 minute. Stir in the shrimp and chili sauce, then reduce the heat and simmer for 1–2 minutes, or until just heated through.

Meanwhile, cook the noodles in a pan of lightly salted boiling water for 4–5 minutes or according to the package directions, until just tender. Drain and return to the pan.

Heat the remaining oil in a small, nonstick skillet, then add the garlic and stir-fry over high heat for 30 seconds. Add to the drained noodles with half the cilantro and toss together until well mixed.

Transfer the chili-and-shrimp mixture to serving dishes and sprinkle over the remaining cilantro. Serve immediately with the garlic noodles.

Shrimp with Scallions & Straw Mushrooms

SERVES 4

- 2 tbsp vegetable or peanut oil
- 1 bunch of scallions, chopped
- 2 garlic cloves, finely chopped
- 1¼ cups coconut cream
- 2 tbsp Thai red curry paste
- 1 cup fish stock
- 2 tbsp Thai fish sauce
- 2 tbsp Thai soy sauce
- 6 fresh Thai basil sprigs
- 14 oz/400 g canned straw mushrooms, drained
- 12 oz/350 g large cooked peeled shrimp
- freshly cooked jasmine rice, to serve

Heat the oil in a wok and stir-fry the scallions and garlic for 2–3 minutes. Add the coconut cream, curry paste, and stock and bring just to a boil.

Stir in the fish sauce and soy sauce, then add the basil, mushrooms, and shrimp. Gradually bring to a boil, then serve immediately with jasmine rice.

vegetable **dishes**

Red Curry
with Mixed Leaves

SERVES 4

2 tbsp peanut or vegetable oil
2 onions, thinly sliced
1 bunch of fine asparagus spears
1¾ cups coconut milk
2 tbsp Thai red curry paste
3 fresh kaffir lime leaves
8 oz/225 g baby spinach leaves
2 heads of bok choy, chopped
1 small head of Chinese cabbage, shredded
handful of fresh cilantro, chopped
freshly cooked rice, to serve

Heat the oil in a preheated wok. Add the onions and asparagus and stir-fry over medium–high heat for 1–2 minutes. Add the coconut milk, curry paste, and lime leaves and bring gently to a boil, stirring occasionally.

Add the spinach, bok choy, and Chinese cabbage and cook, stirring, for 2–3 minutes, or until wilted. Add the cilantro and stir well. Serve immediately with rice.

Eggplant
Curry

SERVES 2

- 2 eggplants, cut into 3/4-inch/2-cm cubes
- 2 tbsp peanut or vegetable oil, plus extra for deep-frying
- 1 bunch of scallions, coarsely chopped
- 2 garlic cloves, chopped
- 2 red bell peppers, seeded and cut into 3/4-inch/2-cm chunks
- 3 zucchini, thickly sliced
- 1 3/4 cups coconut milk
- 2 tbsp Thai red curry paste
- large handful of fresh cilantro, chopped, plus extra leaves to garnish

Heat the oil for deep-frying in a wok, deep pan, or deep-fat fryer to 350–375°F/180–190°C, or until a cube of bread browns in 30 seconds. Add the eggplant cubes, in batches, and cook for 45 seconds–1 minute, or until crisp. Remove with a slotted spoon and drain on paper towels.

Heat the 2 tablespoons of oil in a separate preheated wok or large skillet. Add the scallions and garlic and stir-fry over medium–high heat for 1 minute. Add the bell peppers and zucchini and stir-fry for 2–3 minutes. Add the coconut milk and curry paste and bring gently to a boil, stirring occasionally. Add the eggplants and chopped cilantro, then reduce the heat and simmer for 2–3 minutes. Serve immediately, garnished with cilantro leaves.

Butternut Squash
Curry

SERVES 4

2 tbsp peanut or vegetable oil
1 tsp cumin seeds
2 red onions, sliced
2 celery stalks, sliced
1 large butternut squash, peeled, seeded, and cut into chunks
2 tbsp Thai green curry paste
1¼ cups vegetable stock
2 fresh kaffir lime leaves
⅓ cup fresh bean sprouts
handful of fresh cilantro, chopped, to garnish
freshly cooked rice, to serve

Heat the oil in a preheated wok, then add the cumin seeds and stir-fry over medium–high heat for 2–3 minutes, or until they start to pop. Add the onions and celery and stir-fry for 2–3 minutes. Stir in the squash and stir-fry for an additional 3–4 minutes. Add the curry paste, stock, and lime leaves and bring to a boil, stirring occasionally.

Reduce the heat and simmer gently for 3–4 minutes, or until the squash is tender. Add the bean sprouts and cook for an additional 1–2 minutes, or until warmed through but still crunchy. Sprinkle the cilantro over the curry and serve with rice.

Mixed Vegetables

with Quick-Fried Basil

SERVES 4

2 tbsp vegetable or peanut oil, plus extra for shallow-frying
2 garlic cloves, chopped
1 onion, sliced
4 oz/115 g baby corn, cut in half diagonally
½ cucumber, peeled, halved, seeded, and sliced
8 oz/225 g canned water chestnuts, drained and rinsed
¾ cup snow peas, trimmed
2 cups shiitake mushrooms, halved
1 red bell pepper, seeded and thinly sliced
1 tbsp jaggery or light brown sugar
2 tbsp Thai soy sauce
1 tbsp Thai fish sauce
1 tbsp rice vinegar
8–12 sprigs fresh Thai basil
freshly cooked rice, to serve

Heat the 2 tablespoons of oil in a wok and stir-fry the garlic and onion for 1–2 minutes. Add the corn, cucumber, water chestnuts, snow peas, mushrooms, and bell pepper, and stir-fry for 2–3 minutes, until starting to soften. Add the jaggery, soy sauce, fish sauce, and vinegar, and gradually bring to a boil. Let simmer for 1–2 minutes.

Meanwhile, heat enough oil for shallow-frying in a wok and, when hot, add the basil sprigs. Cook for 20–30 seconds, until crisp. Remove with a slotted spoon and drain on paper towels. Garnish the vegetable stir-fry with the crispy basil and serve immediately with rice.

Crispy Vegetable *Stir-Fry Salad*

SERVES 4

- 2 tbsp peanut or vegetable oil
- 1 bunch of scallions, coarsely chopped
- 1-inch/2.5-cm piece fresh ginger, finely chopped
- 2 lemongrass stalks, halved
- 2 carrots, cut into thin sticks
- 1 small head of broccoli, cut into florets
- 2 oz/55 g baby corn, halved lengthwise
- 2 oz/55 g canned water chestnuts, drained
- 1 tbsp Thai red curry paste
- 8 oz/225 g medium egg noodles
- 4 tbsp sesame seeds
- salt

Heat the oil in a preheated wok. Add the scallions, ginger, and lemongrass and stir-fry over medium–high heat for 2–3 minutes, or until starting to soften. Add the carrots, broccoli, and baby corn and stir-fry for 3–4 minutes, until starting to soften. Add the water chestnuts and curry paste and stir well, then stir-fry for an additional 2–3 minutes. Discard the lemongrass.

Meanwhile, cook the noodles in a large pan of lightly salted boiling water for 4–5 minutes or according to the package directions, until just tender. Drain and return to the pan. Add the sesame seeds and toss to coat. Add the noodles to the stir-fried vegetables and serve immediately.

Hot & Sour Noodle Salad
with Mushrooms

SERVES 4

9 oz/250 g thin rice noodles
2 tbsp sesame oil
6 scallions
6 oz/175 g button mushrooms
½ cucumber, cut into matchsticks

Dressing

4 tbsp sesame oil
2 tbsp Thai fish sauce
juice of 2 limes
1 tsp sugar
1–2 tsp hot chili sauce
2 tbsp chopped fresh cilantro

Soak the noodles in a bowl of hot water for 10–15 minutes or according to the package directions, until tender. Drain and place in a large bowl. Add the oil and toss until the noodles are coated with the oil. Slice the scallions and mushrooms, then add to the noodles together with the cucumber and toss again.

To make the dressing, place the oil, fish sauce, lime juice, sugar, and chili sauce in a small bowl and mix together. Stir in the cilantro. Pour the dressing over the salad and toss until coated. Serve immediately.